Lapps — Reindeer Herders of Lapland

The Lapps have lived in the northern part of Scandinavia, which we call Lapland, for thousands of years. Their nomadic lives remained the same for centuries — they herded reindeer, fished, hunted and grew crops during the short summers. With the arrival of the missionaries in the seventeenth century their way of life began to change, and since that time there has been a constant stream of traders and settlers to their lands. Traditional patterns of life have changed greatly in recent years with new methods of reindeer herding and the arrival of modern technology and tourists. Dr. Alan James has traveled widely in Lapland and assisted with the construction of buildings in the Lapp Museum at Inari. In this book he explains how and why changes are occurring and examines whether the Lapp culture will be able to keep its separate identity while at the same time adapting to the pressures and ways of life of the dominant European culture.

Original Peoples

LAPPS
REINDEER HERDERS OF LAPLAND

Alan James

Rourke Publications, Inc.
Vero Beach, FL 32964

Original Peoples

Eskimos — The Inuit of the Arctic
Maoris of New Zealand
Aborigines of Australia
Plains Indians of North America
South Pacific Islanders
Indians of the Andes
Indians of the Amazon
Bushmen of the Kalahari
Pygmies of Central Africa
Bedouin — The Nomads of the Desert
The Zulus of Southern Africa
Lapps — Reindeer Herders of Lapland

Dedicated to Professor Peter Collison

Frontispiece *Lapp herdsmen take a break during the spring migration.*

Library of Congress Cataloging-in-Publication Data

James, Alan, 1943–
   Lapps : reindeer herders of Lapland / Alan James.
     p.   cm.—(Original peoples)
   Reprint. Originally published: Hove, East Sussex,
England : Wayland, 1985.
   Bibliography: p.
   Includes index
   Summary: Introduces these ancient European people
of northern Scandinavia, describing their culture today
and the adjustments they have made from earlier
times.
   ISBN 0–86625–263–0
   1. Lapps—Juvenile literature. [1. Lapps.]
I. Title.   II. Series.
[DL42.L36J35 1989]
948′.0049455—dc19

                  88–15069
                    CIP
                    AC

Manufactured in Italy.

Text © 1989 Rourke Publications, Inc.

Contents

Introduction

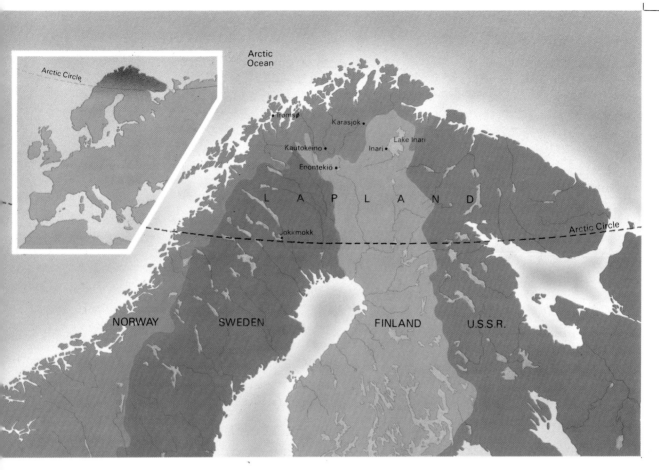

The Lapps live in the north of Scandinavia, in the northern parts of Norway, Sweden, Finland and in a small part of the USSR. Lapland is not a separate country. It is simply a name for the area north of the Arctic Circle where the reindeer-herding Lapps live. It extends from the Kola Peninsula in the USSR to the Atlantic coast of Norway. The name Lapp comes from a Finnish word, *lappalainen*, meaning people of Lapland.

Lapland is a land of contrasts. Eastern Lapland is fairly low lying, but to the west there are mountains, hills and plains. The landscape is covered with huge forests of pine, spruce and birch. Winding lakes and fast-flowing rivers rage in spring when the snow melts.

Winters in Lapland are long and cold, with temperatures as low as −22°F (−30°C). Temperatures can stay below zero for much of the year, and there can be snow on the ground for seven months.

Crops can be grown only during the short summers when daytime temperatures reach 80°F (27°C). Many kinds of wild berries are gathered. The cloudberry is sweet, golden-colored and grows in summer; there are blueberries and cranberries in the autumn.

Bears are now rare, but Arctic foxes, wolverines, eagles and lynx are quite common. All of these can be a danger to the reindeer. There are salmon and trout in rivers and lakes throughout Lapland.

This book explains what life was like for the Lapps in the past, when they herded their reindeer and built temporary homes from branches and skins as they moved from place to place. It also describes how the Lapps live today and the problems that will face them in the future.

Modern lifestyles have now caught up with most Lapps. Many of them own well-equipped homes, cars, snowmobiles, watches, televisions, fashionable as well as traditional clothes, and think nothing of taking a flight from the nearest airport.

A Lapp encampment. Lapps put the finishing touches to their tent.

Chapter 1 **An ancient people**

The early Lapps

The Lapps are one of the oldest and most interesting of the European tribes. These small, sturdy people have lived in this part of north-western Europe for many centuries, always passing on to their children their native skills and customs.

Their early history is lost in antiquity, although it seems likely that the ancestors of present day Lapps lived as wandering nomads in this part of Europe as many as ten thousand years ago. An ancient ski stick and a pair of skis believed to be 4,000 years old have been found in Sweden. This ski stick was one of the spade-ended variety with which a Lapp herdsman dug away the snow to help his reindeer in their search for food. It would indicate that reindeer breeding goes back a very long time indeed.

The early Lapps were hunters of wild reindeer and began to use semi-domesticated reindeer as pack animals. Sometimes, when wild reindeer approached the tame reindeer, they were lassoed by waiting hunters, who may have been dressed in reindeer skins to avoid being noticed.

Many ethnologists believe that the Lapps came from central Russia. There is a connection between the Lappish language and the language of ancient hunting and fishing tribes in Russia. There are also similar racial characteristics among Lapps, Mongols and the Alpine races of Central Europe. Possibly the Lapps moved northwestward into Lapland, while the Mongols moved eastward. Other experts believe the Lapps are simply the primitive and original population of northern Scandinavia, and that they did not arrive from anywhere else.

We know from place names, archaeological remains and folklore

Seventeenth-century illustrations showing Norwegian Lapps.

A Laplander travelling over the Snow.

A Laplander on his Sledge drawn by a Rain-Deer.

that long ago the Lapp settlements extended much farther south, to the forests of Finland and Sweden. Close to Helsinki, the capital of Finland, is a place named Lapinlahti, which means Lapp Bay.

An early photograph of a Lapp family. The Lapp woman holds her baby in a cradle made from reindeer skin.

9

Early records

The Roman historian, Tacitus, made the first written reference to the Lapps. Writing in about A.D. 100, he described the Lapps as *Fenni* — a name by which they are still known in Norway. Tacitus wrote that the *Fenni* were wild and poor, without settled homes, and that they hunted wild animals.

A hoard of gold and silver jewelry discovered in Norwegian Lapland has been dated to the sixth and seventh centuries and suggests that some Lapps were wealthy.

There was little written about the Lapps for many centuries, but at the close of the eighth century a monk named Paulus Diaconus from Lombardy — (now part of northern Italy) — described the Lapps. He said that the name was derived from a word in their language which means "to run." He was describing their speed on skis.

In the ninth century, Othere, a Norwegian official, boasted to King Alfred of England that he owned six hundred tame deer called *rhanas*. These reindeer would probably have been tended by Lapps.

Before they became hunters, Lapps simply followed the reindeer, hunting them with lassoes, bows and arrows, and spears. This picture, dated 1555, shows a Lapp woman accompanying the menfolk on a hunt.

The name *Lappia* was not written until the early thirteenth century, when a Danish monk wrote of a wild area in which men hunted with arrows and spears and lived in tents. The Lapps themselves preferred to be called *Same*. At one time the Lapps disliked the word "Lapp," but it is now commonly used.

From time to time other historians mentioned Lapland and wrote unkindly and in an exaggerated way

A large herd of reindeer heading for the summer pastures.

about the Lapps, describing them as having one eye and living underground in winter!

For centuries, Lapp traditions were not written down but passed verbally from one generation to the next. The written language was first used in the seventeenth century.

Chapter 2 **Influence of outsiders**

A Lapp herdsman heats his kettle over a log fire. Lapp tents are open at the top to let the smoke escape.

Missionaries

For hundreds of years the Lapps lived their lives free from outside interference. Then, in the seventeenth century, Christian missionaries began to make their way north into Lapland. In 1619, a prayer book in Lappish was printed in Stockholm, the earliest book printed in the Lapp language. The New Testament appeared in Lappish in 1755, and in 1811 the entire Bible was translated into Lappish.

A missionary named Knud Leem went to Norwegian Lapland in 1725 and spent the rest of his life among the Lapps. He wrote of the watery eyes of many Lapps, attributing this to the tents filled with smoke from their fires, as well as to the bright dazzle of sunlight on the snow.

In 1752 a college was founded at Trondheim in Norway, where missionaries were taught the Lapp language. A century later another missionary, Lars Laestadius, arrived in Lapland and began a fiercely puritan campaign. He considered that festivals, old songs and decorative clothing were sinful. Many songs and legends were lost as a result of his efforts to stamp out the old way of life.

Once missionaries were able to speak Lappish they began to realize how varied were the religious beliefs held by these people. Their practices included bear worship, for the Lapps regarded the bear as a sacred animal.

They also believed that at the beginning of a journey the spirit of the traveler often went on ahead to let others know he was arriving, or to give other information about him.

A *shaman* was a Lapp magician who had powerful magic drums that the Lapps feared. A *shaman* claimed to be able to look into the future with the aid of these drums. Sometimes *shamans* were caught by Christian missionaries and burned alive with their drums.

Lapps used to believe in many gods and goddesses similar to the old Viking gods. Here, a Lapp worships the image of Tiermes (or Thor) on a sacred plot behind his hut.

Traders and settlers

Over the centuries, the Lapps began to adapt their way of life to new ideas brought into Lapland. Missionaries, local sheriffs, pioneer settlers, fishermen, trappers and traders all began coming north. Finnish traders set up a fur trade with the Lapps. The Scandinavian countries gradually extended control and political power over Lapland and the lives of the Lapps.

During the seventeenth century, silver was discovered in the mountains of Swedish Lapland. Sweden at that time was not a wealthy country, so efforts were made to mine the silver ore. The Lapps and their reindeer were used to transport the ore down the mountains.

A herdsman nails reindeer skins up to dry. The Lapps traded reindeer skins for other goods.

In 1751 Sweden and Norway agreed on the exact location of their national border. However, the Lapps were still allowed to move freely across the border between one country and another and to use the land on either side of the frontier to feed themselves and their reindeer. The border between Norway and Russia was fixed in 1826.

Hunters and fishermen often tried to take over parts of the traditional areas used by the Lapps. The various governments hoped that the Lapps and the settlers would be able to live peacefully in the same area, with the Lapps herding reindeer, hunting and fishing, and the settlers farming. But the Lapps found that they began to lose some of their land, and this caused difficulties.

Lapp herdsmen, following their reindeer, were allowed to move freely from country to country.

Seasonal gatherings

The Lapps, from ancient times, have been subject to different types of taxation. At one time, those living in the very far north had to pay taxes to Norway, Sweden and Russia, but eventually the taxation of the Lapps came under government control.

The early tax collectors traded with the Lapps for the skins of

beaver and squirrel, as well as for meat, fish, seal, whale and walrus. The markets still held by the Lapps in the spring are reminders of the days when they had to journey to central villages in order to pay their taxes. At these places trading developed.

The Lapps were more or less defenseless against government edicts. They were often treated unfairly and there was little they could do in retaliation. They lived scattered and often isolated lives. This was one reason why a separate "Lapp Country" was never formed. Several ancient writers mentioned Lapp kings, but these were almost certainly legendary characters.

After a long and possibly lonely winter, reindeer herders and their families looked forward to visiting the nearest village. This spring trip gave them the chance to wear their best clothes, to meet acquaintances and to have a well-deserved break from routine.

Lapp weddings often took place at these tribal gatherings. The bride received one ring on becoming engaged, a second ring when the marriage took place and a third ring when the first male child was born. All these rings were identical.

A Lapp wedding. Although Lapps have been Christians now for several centuries, the marriage ceremony retains many old customs.

Reindeer racing at the Lapp settlement of Kautokeino.

These seasonal get-togethers provided an opportunity to buy food and utensils from the store. Sports were also enjoyed, for even when the Lapps were relaxing they still gained much pleasure and amusement from their reindeer. The sports included ski joring (being pulled along on skis by a reindeer), reindeer-lassoing competitions, and reindeer-racing contests using sleds. These races are still held at Easter in the Lapp villages of Karasjok and Kautokeino in Norway.

Chapter 3 **Herders of reindeer**

Reindeer migrations

Reindeer have always been of vital importance to the Lapp economy. At one time they fed, clothed and housed the Lapps, and it used to be claimed with much truth that when the reindeer died out the Lapp community would die out as well.

A reindeer, or *poro*, to use the Lapp word, stands about 3 feet (1 meter) high at the shoulder. It has small ears and a short tail. The hooves are broad and the foot spreads out on the ground to give a sure foothold on ice and snow. The antlers give the animal its apparent large size. Both bucks (males) and does (females) have antlers, but those of the males are larger and branching. Antlers are shed every year. The male has an addition to its antlers, called a brow-tine, with which it searches for moss and

When their reindeer moved on in search of food, Lapp herders packed up their tents to follow them.

lichen. Reindeer also use their antlers to attack other animals, but for much of the year the antlers are small, delicate and too fragile to be used for fighting.

Until the early twentieth century, a Lapp family would follow its herd of reindeer fairly closely. When the reindeer moved in search of food, the family would pack up its tent and few belongings, load them on the backs of pack reindeer and follow the herd.

A herdsman leads his reindeer across a wide lake to reach summer pastures.

The reindeers' journey to the hills after winter must take place before ice-covered rivers and lakes thaw. Reindeer do not like to get wet and they will only attempt to swim if it becomes essential while they are on migration. Usually, migration routes are the same every year and it is very unusual for reindeer to deviate from them.

19

Summer camps

In summer and autumn many Lapp families used to live scattered lives. They had to find pasture for their reindeer, which were in desperate need of grass after eating nothing but lichen during the long winter. By the end of June, irritating mosquitoes drove the reindeer from the forests to the fells above the treeline. The Lapps fished, hunted and gathered together a store of food for the winter months. The reindeer were usually allowed to roam freely, and the family lived in a large tent, which would be pitched at the limit of the tree line. This gave them access to fuel and a clear view of the pastures.

Tents varied in construction but all were simple, having two semi-circular bands of wood that made a central framework. Birch poles were placed around this main support and

A reindeer grazing in the forest.

A Lapp family and their dog beside their tent. Lapps often used dogs to help them control their reindeer herds.

were covered with several reindeer skins or canvas sheets hooked in place with a long pole. The top of the tent was left open to allow smoke from the fire to escape. The Lapp was an expert at quickly taking down his tent and putting it up again, since it might be pulled down and set up elsewhere several times each year.

Nomadic Lapps had very few possessions — a family tent, a sawing-horse standing outside the tent on which fuel was cut up for the fire, a few knives shaped in such a way that they could also be used as axes, a simple food safe to protect food from prowling animals, and inside the tent perhaps a chest containing utensils or clothing.

There were no fixed mealtimes. Everything depended on the weather and the mood of the reindeer. Meat was kept in a pot ready to be boiled.

21

Winter villages

Reindeer were able to graze on the open fells until autumn, but when the snow began to fall they migrated to the forest areas. There the snow was less deep than on the bare hills, and therefore lichen could be found more easily.

Winter is a hard time for reindeer. Using their brow-tines, bucks scrape away snow and try to find food to survive. After older bucks have shed their antlers in November they must use their hooves to paw away the snow. Young bucks keep their antlers until February and the does until spring. Reindeer drink in winter by eating snow.

During winter the women and girls used to live in a log cabin in a settlement called a *visten*, while the men and boys lived in a small tent called a *laavu*, as they followed the herd around. Life in a winter settlement was cramped, and often one small log cabin served for all purposes. The herders seldom visited the settlement and their visits were short — usually just to bring meat or to collect bread.

When snow is as deep as 3 feet (1 meter), reindeer are unable to reach the moss below and may starve. If ice

In winter the reindeer have to scrape away the snow with their hooves to find lichen and moss on which to feed.

A Lapp boy and his mother outside their laavu.

forms a frozen crust on the snow, the reindeer cannot reach the moss. When this happens the Lapps can do little to help and they must allow the animals to take care of themselves by nibbling at the lichen on the barks of trees. If there is only a thin layer of snow, the reindeer tend to roam too freely and to spread out over wide areas. One and a half to two feet (50–60 centimeters) of snow is preferred by the Lapps, since at this depth the herds tend to stay together and the animals can manage to find food.

Food, clothing and utensils

Until fairly recently, life for a nomad was often very difficult. Food, warmth and shelter were the only things that really mattered. In winter, snow had to be melted to get water for cooking or for the traditional morning drink of coffee. Firewood was needed in large quantities in winter, and often there was not enough of it.

Above *A Lapp women sews a reindeer-skin moccasin.*

Left *Lapp men in Sweden wear hats with big red pom-poms on top.*

Besides reindeer, some Lapps kept goats to provide milk and cheese. Most Lapps ate reindeer meat and cheese and drank reindeer milk. Canned food, potatoes, cereals and butter had to be obtained from the nearest store, although some Lapps grew rye, barley, potatoes, carrots, and turnips.

Lapps have always been skilled at carving bone, antler and wood. Children's toys were usually made from wood. Pine was used to make sleds, and birch was used for almost every household item — plates, cups, chairs, shelves, tables and beds.

The traditional Lapp costumes are brightly colored and highly decorative. Lapp women used to weave the material on handlooms. Women wear bonnets with flaps to protect their ears. Lapp men in Norway and Finland wear large floppy hats with four points known as the hats of the four winds, while in Sweden they have hats with large red pom-poms. Males in Russian Lapland wear square caps with fur-trimmed borders. The tunic, called a *kolte*, is made of deep blue felt with bands of yellow, red and green and often has colorful embroidery. Trousers narrow at the calf. Moccasins are made from pieces of reindeer skin sewn together. Dry grass is used instead of stockings and is stuffed into the shoe to make a tight, snug fit. "As you line your shoes, so will you walk," goes one old Lapp saying. The grass is dried out at night, ready for the next day. The felt trousers of summer are exchanged in winter for reindeer-skin leggings for extra warmth. Thick gloves are also worn.

A Lapp family in traditional clothing. Notice the "hat of the four winds," the kolte *(tunic) and reindeer-skin coats.*

Chapter 4 **Twentieth-century life**

Changes in reindeer herding

Reindeer were once used by the Lapps as beasts of burden and to provide milk, meat and hides. Now most reindeer are bred simply to be slaughtered and are sold directly to wholesale dealers as complete carcases. Because of this it has become difficult for the Lapps to obtain parts of the reindeer such as internal organs that were once used to store milk, hide to make clothing and utensils, and antlers and bones as raw materials for handicrafts and for making glue. Few reindeer are now milked, and they are seldom harnessed to sleds or used as pack animals.

A Lapp house in the summer pastures.

In autumn the reindeer are rounded up, using lassoes, and put into pens.

Family migrations are now either short or do not occur at all. Most families who keep reindeer have settled down in large villages situated in good pastureland. Some families live in one village all year long, while others live in two locations — one for summer and one for winter. Some may live in three villages — one for summer, one for winter and the third for spring and autumn. Some Lapps now have spacious houses in both summer and winter villages.

During late summer and autumn the reindeer are allowed to roam freely. Now they usually make the migration toward the trees without supervision.

The first snow falls in October, at which time reindeer are rounded up, using lassoes, and enclosed in pens. They are then sorted, and each reindeer owner has his identification mark cut into his reindeer's ears.

The size of a herd varies, but a herd of at least five hundred reindeer is needed to support a family with a reasonable income. Many herds are far smaller.

27

Modern Lapp settlements

The contents of a Lapp's home now differ little from that of any other home in Lapland. The Lapps no longer have to manage on reindeer products. Life has become more sophisticated. The Lapps can choose exactly what they want from stores and pay for it with money instead of having to use their ingenuity to make things for themselves.

A Lapp woman sews the hem of her dress. An electric sewing machine makes her task easy.

Jokkmokk in Swedish Lapland. It was around 1600 when nomadic Lapps built the first houses here as a winter base.

When homes were simpler, it was necessary for the Lapps to wear thick clothing to protect themselves against the biting cold. Now that the home of a typical Lapp is very similar, or even identical, to that of the other residents of northern Scandinavia, keeping out the cold means improving the type of house rather than wearing thicker clothes.

The living conditions of many Lapps were at one time made difficult by bad roads, lack of electricity and long distances from one place to another. In the late 1970s, roads were improved in many parts of Lapland and most houses can now be reached by car. These days the majority of Lapp homes have electricity, and those without commercial electricity use portable power generators.

There have been marked improvements in the housing conditions of the Lapps over the last few years. The Lapps now have dwellings that reach the standard of the average housing of the entire country.

29

A variety of occupations

Originally, the Lapps lived by hunting, fishing and keeping a few tame reindeer. In the sixteenth century a different kind of occupation developed. Mountain reindeer breeding became popular; this involved seasonal migrations of larger herds in search of food. Many Lapps today earn their living from a combination of reindeer breeding and some other occupation — a similar way of life, in fact, to that found long ago.

About one-third of the Lapps in Finland earn their living solely from reindeer breeding, and a third earn their living from a combination of reindeer breeding, agriculture, fishing and forestry work. The remaining third work in industries, trade or service occupations. This means that two-thirds of the Lapps in

Lapps are now employed in a variety of jobs. This Lapp is a silversmith.

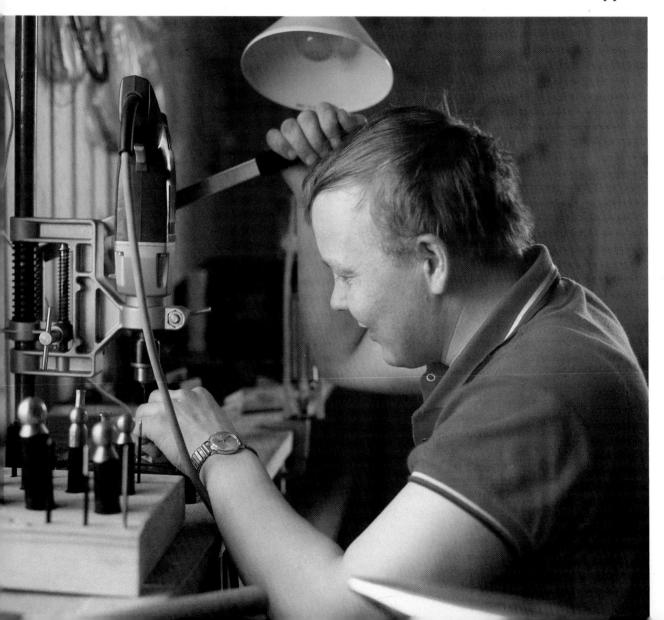

Today, some Lapps do seasonal work. Here, Finnish Lapps are sorting young reindeer into small herds before journeying to winter feeding grounds.

Finland still earn their living through natural resources — reindeer, farming, fishing and forestry. Some Lapps are unemployed.

Over Lapland as a whole, most Lapps earn their livings from work other than reindeer breeding. Lapps are now employed as miners, railroad workers, nurses, assistants in hospitals and schools, office workers, teachers, dentists, doctors, builders and tradesmen. Some Lapps earn their livings by making souvenirs for tourists, while others do seasonal work — reindeer herding during busy periods, such as in the early summer when fawns born that spring are ear-notched. Late autumn and early winter are also busy. This is when the reindeer are sorted into small winter herds so that they can find food more easily before journeying to winter feeding grounds. Fishing and work on iron ore railroads are also seasonal occupations.

31

Lapp children take a ride in a canoe-shaped pulkka.

Traveling around

Because Lapland is so large, methods of travel have always been important. The traditional way to move about in winter was on skis, and Lapps became expert skiers.

There were various types of *pulkka*, which were canoe-shaped sleds with one runner, pulled by a reindeer. The most common *pulkka* seated one adult passenger with legs outstretched ready for breaking. Another *pulkka* was wider and was used to transport baggage and belongings. A third kind was used by the Skolt (originally Russian) Lapps for transporting sick people, children and belongings. Reindeer were harnessed three-abreast to this style of sled.

There were various kinds of sleds, called *reki*, with two runners that were also pulled by reindeer. Reindeer have never been used for riding purposes in Lapland, although a Lapp child may ride a tame reindeer for fun.

Snowmobiles, which are like motorized sleds, were introduced in the early 1960s. They are used for pulling heavy loads, work that was once done by reindeer. The use of snowmobiles has made the rounding up of reindeer, and caring for them, much easier. These vehicles can travel at speeds of up to 50 miles (80 kilometers) per hour. Although such machines have become something of a status symbol, they are too expensive for small-scale reindeer breeders to run and maintain.

The revolution in transportation and communications means that Lapland is no longer remote. There are flights from northern airports to the cities of Scandinavia. Small planes land on frozen lakes, and helicopters are used in emergencies. The improvement of roads has increased the volume of conventional traffic, such as cars, trucks and buses.

The old and the new are shown side by side. Lapps at this encampment use a snowmobile to pull their traditional reki *(sled).*

Tourism

Lapland is currently being promoted by the Scandinavian governments as a splendid place for a holiday. Tourists journey north to ski and to fish, to sail and canoe, to walk on the fells, to climb the mountains or to rest in the peace of unspoiled natural surroundings.

Lapland is an area that attracts tourists all through the year — long days and nights of sunlight when the Midnight Sun shines continually in summer; the beauty of autumn as the leaves turn gold; snow, skiing and the chance to see the Northern Lights during winter; skiing between March and May, known as the time of "spring winter"; and walking among flowers in the late spring.

Right *Lapp boys sell reindeer-skin purses to tourists.*

Below *The sun never sets completely during summer in the far north.*

A tourist industry has been built up to meet the needs of tourists. There are hotels, holiday villages and information centers.

The Lapps have also become involved in tourism. They make Lapp handicrafts that are sold to tourists as souvenirs. These include reindeer-skin slippers, Lapp bonnets and belts, objects made of bone and wood, and knives and medallions bearing ancient Lapp symbols.

Norwegian tourists paying for their sled ride.

They also supply hotels with Lapp delicacies, such as salmon, ptarmigan, grouse and reindeer meat. Reindeer stew, smoked reindeer, steaks and roasts are all popular, as are cloudberries for dessert. Liqueurs are made from cloudberries and cranberries.

Some Lapps work at holiday centers. They may help to run the illuminated slalom ski slopes or, dressed in traditional costumes, organize reindeer driving schools or winter safaris. These safaris cross the fell country on sleds pulled by reindeer or snowmobiles and last for several days. There are also summer safaris by Landrover. It is also possible for tourists to try their luck at panning for gold by the banks of a number of rivers in Lapland.

Chapter 5 **Problems facing Lapland**

Finnish Lapps wearing traditional dress. The women wear bonnets with flaps to protect their ears from the cold.

The Lapp language

The Lapps speak a language known to linguists as Finno-Ugrian, which is closely related to the Finnish language. Because the Lapps have led such scattered lives, as many as nine different Lapp languages have evolved. The three main dialects of Lapp are central, southern and eastern dialects. The central dialect is spoken by the largest number of Lapps and is used in parts of Norway, Sweden and Finland. Various types of central Lappish are spoken in different areas.

The speakers of certain dialects often have great difficulty in communicating with other Lapps. However, most Lapps are now bilingual, speaking both Lappish and the language of the country to which they belong. Some Lapps no longer speak Lappish.

The Lapp word for reindeer herd is *aello*. This literally means "what one lives on." About a quarter of the words in the vocabulary of the central Lappish dialect are concerned with reindeer and the breeding of reindeer. There are words for a reindeer's age and appearance, its color and shade of fur, its size, sex and qualities and even for the shape of its antlers. There is a different word for a male reindeer in each of the first seven years of its life.

Many specialized words exist to describe various types of weather and snow conditions. There is also a host of words for valleys, hills, lakes and rivers — *aedno* is a large river, *jakka* is a small river, *njavvi* is a slowly gliding part of a river, and *goadnil* is a quiet section of river free from currents near the riverbank.

The Torne dialect of northern Lappish, an important variant of central Lappish, has been made the basis of a written Lapp language common to Norway and Sweden.

A forest of antlers — the roundup of a huge herd of reindeer.

Schools

If Lapp children live close enough to a school, they travel there daily, perhaps on skis in winter. If they live far away, the only solution is for them to board during the term and return home on weekends or for the vacations.

In some places there are special Lapp schools in which children learn to read and write the language of the country where they live, as well as a variant of the Lappish tongue. School subjects are much the same the world over, but Lapp children also learn something of Lappish history, art, folklore, the care of reindeer, handicrafts and regional geography — all of which will be of practical use to them in later life. The curriculum of the Lapp schools aims not only to provide a useful course for pupils but also to help them appreciate their special position as people with a double cultural

A classroom photograph taken in 1953, several years after the opening of this winter school for nomadic Lapps in Jokkmokk, Sweden.

heritage — that they are first and foremost Lapps, which is something to be proud of, and of their place in the wider traditions of the country in which they live. These schools are important as they try to conserve traditional attitudes, while at the same time encourage worthwhile change.

Lapp children who do not learn much about their cultural heritage at school will grow up knowing much

Lapp children play on the lake shore, their feet warm and dry in boots bought from the local store.

more about the world outside Lapland than their parents. Since reindeer herding and other traditional Lapp occupations can no longer support the growing population, training for other types of employment is now essential.

39

These houses are Swedish holiday homes built beside one of Lapland's many lakes.

Rising land prices

Lapland covers a vast area of land. There are 30,000 Lapps in Norway, 15,000 in Sweden, 4,000 in Finland and 2,000 in the USSR. This is quite a small population. If the Lapps were the only people who lived in Lapland, the countryside would have a very desolate and empty

appearance. As it is, there have always been Scandinavian traders, settlers and farmers who have journeyed to the north to live and work in Lapland. Today there are hundreds of thousands of Norwegians, Swedes, Finns and Russians living in Lapland and only about 50,000 Lapps.

The Scandinavians living in Lapland — many of whom are descendants of early settlers — tend to live mainly in the larger towns where they have a wide variety of occupations.

Some of the people with property in Lapland are only part-time residents. Many Scandinavian families own a smaller, second home where they spend their vacations. Lapland has become a popular place for vacations now that travel by road, rail and air is so well developed. Indeed, it is amusing to compare these second-home owners with the traditional life of reindeer-herding Lapps — since both groups travel and migrate at specific times of the year.

The rise in popularity of summer cottages in Lapland has resulted in problems for the local people already living there, including, of course, the Lapps. Such part-time residents in Lapland are often wealthy people who can afford to pay far more for land or property than the local people. Recently the value of some land has risen by about 400 percent.

Real estate agents are anxious to sell land for as high a price as possible, which often means that those already living in Lapland stand little chance of buying land. Local people also suffer when a new buyer is granted fishing rights with the land. Traditional reindeer-grazing lands have similarly been reduced by land speculation, increased development along new roads, and the construction of dams and resevoirs.

Forest trees are cut down and sent to a large Swedish paper mill. This is just one of the industries affecting traditional reindeer-grazing lands.

Preserving Lapp culture

In winter, lakes freeze over and the land may be covered by up to 3 feet (1 meter) of snow. However, snowplows keep the main roads clear, and the outside influences of Scandinavian culture continue, even during the perpetual darkness of winter — a time of year the Lapps call *kaamos*, meaning twilight time.

Lapland, with its traditional way of life, is a land in danger. Many changes have occurred already and there are now many competing influences. This makes some Lapps fear that the old way of life will be swallowed up and disappear forever as their people accept new values and standards.

Rapid changes in lifestyle since the 1960s have caused many people to examine whether or not it is possible to retain aspects of the old culture, while at the same time accepting what is beneficial in the culture imported from the wider society.

Schools play an important part in preserving aspects of Lapp culture. The Lapps are an artistic people and

Winter in Kautokeino in Norwegian Lapland. Snowplows keep the main roads open.

A herdsman in his hut in the winter pastures. Convenience foods and a radio have improved his hard and lonely life.

A reconstruction of an old Lapp timber building. It would originally have been covered with turf to keep out drafts.

have been given financial support by various governments to encourage traditional handicrafts. Folk music and folk poetry are receiving more attention and are being recorded for future generations.

There have been regular programs broadcast on the radio for the Lapps in all four of the Lapland countries. The subjects are of interest to the Lapps, and at the same time give the general public a better understanding of the Lapp way of life. News bulletins have also been broadcast in Lappish.

The open-air Lapp Museum at Inari in Finnish Lapland is a center for the study of Lapp life. Lapp buildings and artifacts from the past are preserved or reconstructed, thus providing a permanent record of Lapp achievement.

Groups and societies that study and record life in the past, and encourage the older Lapp ways of life alongside generally changing lifestyles, have helped the Lapps to become members of a wider culture.

43

Chapter 6 The future of the Lapps

Coastal Lapps and reindeer Lapps on Norway's north shore. Some wear parkas and jeans, while others still wear traditional clothes.

Adapting to a modern lifestyle and accepting new values has eased a hard existence for many Lapps living in their hostile environment. There are some Lapps who welcome such changes, whereas others feel threatened and believe they will lose their sense of identity. The Lapp was once respected in the north, but outside influences have resulted in a lessening of the personal standing of older Lapps. Young Lapps now tell

44

the time from digital watches instead of from the sun as their forefathers did. They have bicycles and prefer to wear parkas and jeans instead of traditional clothing, which tends to be worn only on special occasions, if at all.

The third Nordic Lapp Conference, held in 1959, decided that the governments of Scandinavia should jointly study the problems of the Lapp population. The aim of this conference was to make clear what measures needed to be taken to develop the culture of the Lapps and to improve their living conditions. A Lapp parliament now watches over the rights of all Lapps.

It is often said that the Lapps are like their reindeer — both are a little shy and both have tended to prefer the lonely hills. Times are changing and life is becoming more technical.

The economic life of the Lapps has changed from a self-sufficient, natural economy to a monetary economy. Many Lapps are becoming more prosperous and have more comfortable housing with a less difficult and possibly healthier lifestyle. As better educated citizens, they are able to shape their own futures more effectively. Such factors encourage many of them to face the future with optimism.

A Lapp family crosses the icy wastes on snowmobile and sled.

Glossary

Antlers Branching horns that grow from a reindeer's head. They are shed annually. The reindeer is the only member of the deer family in which both males and females have antlers.

Artifacts Things made by human workmanship, such as tools.

Bilingual Someone who speaks two languages.

Dialect A form of speech peculiar to a particular group of people or district.

Edict An order issued by those in authority.

Ethnologist A person who studies different human races, especially their characteristics, customs and relationships to one another.

Fells Rolling hills, mountains or moors.

Folklore Traditional beliefs of a group of people.

Identification marks A method of marking so that a reindeer owner can spot his own animals and know to whom other animals belong.

Lappish The language of the Lapps.

Lichen A plant, usually gray, green or yellow, that grows on rocks and tree-trunks.

Liqueur A strong, sweet alcoholic drink.

Midnight Sun At 70° latitude the sun does not set for 73 days, from mid-May until the end of July, giving light for twenty-four hours each day.

Migration A movement from one place to another depending on the season.

Missionaries People who attempt to convert others to a religious belief.

Moccasins Footwear made of animal skin.

Monetary economy A way of life based on buying and selling by using money.

Natural economy A way of life based on providing for one's own needs by keeping animals or growing crops.

Nomadic Traveling from one place to another to find pasture and food.

Northern Lights Colored lights seen in the sky in northern countries in winter, caused by the sun sending out electrified particles. Astronomers call them aurora borealis, meaning northern dawn.

Panning Washing soil and gravel in a pan to separate particles of valuable minerals.

Parliament An assembly of the representatives of a political nation or people.

Ptarmigan A bird of the grouse family.

Puritan A word describing a person who is strict in religion and morality.

Religion A system of beliefs. Most Lapps follow Lutheran Christianity.

Rhanas An early spelling of "reindeer." Other early words were "raindeer" and "range deer" — suggesting free movement of herds during grazing.

Service occupations Jobs that entail looking after others or providing a "service" rather than making something.

Skolt Lapps A group of Lapps dispersed from Russia after the 1939-45 war when national borders were changed. They now live in Finnish Lapland. Their religion is Greek Orthodox.

Slalom A ski race with obstacles placed on the course.

Speculation Investment in the hope of making more money.

Status symbol A possession that is regarded as proof of the owner's wealth, importance or social position.

Transition The change from one state or stage to another.

Verbally By spoken (rather than written) word.

Glossary of Lapp words

Aedno   A large river.

Aello   A reindeer herd.

Fenni   A word used by Norwegian Lapps to describe themselves.

Goadnil   A quiet stretch of river free from currents near a riverbank.

Jakka   A small river.

Kaamos   The twilight period of snow and winter darkness.

Kolte   A blue felt tunic worn by Lapps.

Laavu   A small tent once used by part of the family in winter when following reindeer on migration.

Njavvi   Part of a river that glides slowly.

Poro   A general word for reindeer (but there are very many others).

Pulkka   A canoe-shaped sled with one runner that is pulled by a reindeer.

Reki   An ordinary type of sled with two runners.

Same   A word the Lapps use to describe themselves, often used instead of the word "Lapp."

Shaman   A Lapp magician believed to have special and secret powers. He had an oval drum on which drawings were sketched with red dye. Rings were placed on a drawing of the sun and the drum was beaten. The rings jumped and settled on some of the other drawings, and the *shaman* was believed to use the position of the rings to look into the future.

Visten   Lapp settlements of permanent buildings, perhaps used all year long or for just part of the year.

Books to read

The Lapps by Roberto Basi (Greenwood, 1960).

The Skolt Lapps Today by Tim Ingold (Cambridge University Press, 1977).

The Finns and the Lapps: How They Live and Work by John L. Irwin (HR&W, 1973).

Lapps and Scandinavians: Archaeological Finds from Northern Sweden by Inger Zachrisson (Coronet Books, 1976).

Norway's Reindeer Lapps by Sally Anderson (National Geographic, Vol. 152, No. 3, September, 1977).

The Lapps by Bjorn Collinder (Princeton, 1949).

Finland by William Graves (National Geographic, Vol. 133, No. 5, May, 1968).

Let's Visit Finland by Alan James (Burke, 1979).

The Nomadism of the Swedish Mountain Lapps by Ernst Manker (Stockholm, 1953).

People of Eight Seasons by Ernst Manker (Nordbok, 1975).

Coast Lapp Society by Robert Paine (Tromso, 1957).

The Lapps in Sweden by Johan Turi (Stockholm, 1910).

Social Relations in a Nomadic Lapp Community by Ian Whitaker (Oslo, 1955).

Index

Picture acknowledgments

The illustrations in this book were supplied by the following: Bryan and Cherry Alexander *cover, frontispiece*, 7, 11, 12, 14, 15, 16, 17, 18, 19, 20, 22, 23, 24 (left), 25, 26, 27, 28, 30, 33, 34 (left), 35, 39, 42, 43, 45; Embassy of Finland 31, 36; Mary Evans Picture Library 8, 10, 21; GEOSLIDES Photo Library 24 (right), 34 (right); Alan James 43; Mansell Collection 9; TOPHAM 13, 29, 32, 37, 38; Wayland Picture Library 40, 41. The map on page 6 was drawn by Bill Donohoe.
© Copyright 1986 Wayland (Publishers) Ltd
61 Western Road, Hove, East Sussex, BN3 1JD England